POCKET
BOOKS

BY KEN BLANCHARD

Full Steam Ahead! *(with Jesse Stoner), 2003*
The One Minute® Apology: A Powerful Way to Make Things Better
(with Margaret McBride), 2003
Zap the Gaps!: Target Higher Performance and Achieve It
(with Dana Gaines Robinson and James C. Robinson), 2002
Whale Done!: The Power of Positive Relationships
(with Thad Lacinak, Chuck Tompkins and Jim Ballard), 2002
High Five! *(with Sheldon Bowles), 2001*
Management of Organizational Behavior: Utilizing Human Resources
(with Paul Hersey), 8th edition, 2000
Big Bucks! *(with Sheldon Bowles), 2000*
Leadership by the Book *(with Bill Hybels and Phil Hodges), 1999*
The Heart of a Leader, *1999*
Gung Ho! *(with Sheldon Bowles), 1998*
Raving Fans: A Revolutionary Approach to Customer Service
(with Sheldon Bowles), 1993
Management by Values *(with Michael O'Connor), 1997*
Mission Possible *(with Terry Waghorn), 1996*
Empowerment Takes More Than a Minute
(with John P. Carlos and Alan Randolph), 1996
Everyone's a Coach *(with Dan Shula), 1995*
We Are the Beloved, *1994*
Playing the Great Game of Golf: Making Every Minute Count, *1992*
The One Minute Manager® Builds High Performing Teams
(with Don Carew and Eunice Parisi-Carew), 1990
The One Minute Manager® Meets the Monkey
(with William Oncken, Jr., and Hal Burrows), 1989
The Power of Ethical Management *(with Norman Vincent Peale), 1988*
The One Minute Manager® Gets Fit
(with D.W. Edington and Marjorie Blanchard), 1986
Leadership and the One Minute Manager®
(with Patricia Zigarmi and Drea Zigarmi), 1985
Organizational Change Through Effective Leadership
(with Robert H. Guest and Paul Hersey), 2nd edition, 1985
Putting the One Minute Manager® to Work *(with Robert Lorber), 1984*
The One Minute Manager® *(with Spencer Johnson), 1982*
The Family Game: A Situational Approach to Effective Parenting
(with Paul Hersey), 1979

BY MARC MUCHNICK

**Naked Management: Bare Essentials for Motivating the
X-Generation at Work,** *1996*

The Leadership Pill

*The Missing Ingredient in
Motivating People Today*

Ken Blanchard
Marc Muchnick

POCKET
BOOKS

New York • London • Toronto • Sydney

This edition first published by Pocket Books, 2004
An imprint of Simon & Schuster UK Ltd
A Viacom Company

1 3 5 7 9 10 8 6 4 2

Simon & Schuster UK Ltd
Africa House
64–78 Kingsway
London WC2B 6AH

www.simonsays.co.uk

Simon & Schuster Australia
Sydney

A CIP catalogue record for this book is available from the British Library

ISBN 0-7434-8387-1

Printed and in Great Britain by
Cox & Wyman Ltd, Reading, Berkshire

*We dedicate this book to the
Blanchard and Muchnick family leaders,
past and present.*

*To our inspirational wives,
Margie Blanchard and Kim Muchnick.*

*To our posterity,
Scott Blanchard and Debbie Blanchard Medina,
Kurtis and Kyle Blanchard,
Jessica and Blake Muchnick.*

*To our extended family members,
Humberto Medina, Tom McKee, Mark Manning,
Adam and Cynthia Muchnick, William Moreland,
Nicole and Matt Benak.*

CONTENTS

INTRODUCTION

Today's workforce is more sophisticated, diverse, and informed than ever before. As a result, the "my way or the highway" command-and-control approach to management doesn't cut it anymore. Ultimately, people are looking for something different—and better—in organizational leadership. They demand leaders who not only get results, but who win the trust and respect of their teams.

The Leadership Pill is a fun parable that underscores the need for leaders to show integrity, build a culture of partnership, and affirm people's sense of self-worth by letting them know that what they do is important. Our belief is that when you tune in to what people really want, you can outperform anyone—even someone who thinks they have found the perfect Leadership Pill.

We hope you will read this book to discover what it really takes to become an Effective Leader, and then perhaps share it with others who will benefit from the powerful message and learning points it contains. Remember, leadership is not something you do *to* people, it's something you do *with* them.

Our very best,
Ken and Marc
San Diego, California

The Leadership Pill

THE DISCOVERY

One sunny day in Corporate America, Leadership Pill Industries (LPI) opened their first production facility with an announcement that received immediate national media coverage: "We can compress all of the attributes of effective leadership into a single pill."

Years of research and pilot studies had finally paid off. The company appropriately named their groundbreaking product the Leadership Pill and made plans to mass-market it across the land.

The Leadership Pill was viewed by the press as an especially stunning innovation. After lamenting the shortage of talented leaders in business, politics, and other organizational circles, the media clamored for more information.

"Industry survey data readily supports the launch of the Leadership Pill," the LPI spokesperson reported.

In an effort to further define the market for their new product, Leadership Pill Industries hired an independent agency to conduct a series of focus groups to explore various important questions. One question in particular evoked the liveliest response from most participants: **"Of all the leaders you have met, how many of them do you consider to be truly *great* leaders?"**

"The focus group data is compelling," LPI reported to the media upon receiving and analyzing the results. "CEOs and vice presidents across the board are concerned with the lack of leadership depth within their ranks, especially at the middle management level. Only a few front-line supervisors and employees recall feeling like they have ever worked for a truly great leader."

Case studies conducted by industrial psychologists at a national leadership think tank also substantiated these findings.

"The majority of business, government, and nonprofit organizations are stuck in a perpetual leadership crisis," the agency's white paper revealed. "On top of this, stress and job insecurity continue to pervade the business landscape. There are no signs that the situation is likely to change going forward."

Mounting anticipation of the Leadership Pill's arrival set off a wave of excitement. Company boardrooms bustled with anticipation. Employees speculated at the watercooler. No one could believe it—leadership in a pill!

"But can the Leadership Pill rid the world of micromanagers and overbearing executives?" many asked. "Is there truly hope that leaders might actually do what they say?"

It was a delightfully tempting proposition, they reasoned.

While support for the Leadership Pill was tremendous, one prominent and well-regarded figure in organizational leadership—aptly known as the Effective Leader based on his proven abilities over the years—raised a strong note of caution.

"If they don't have the right blend of leadership ingredients, the Leadership Pill will do more damage than good," the Effective Leader stated in a talk-show interview.

THE PRESS CONFERENCE

In response to the attention that the Leadership Pill was receiving, the director of public relations at Leadership Pill Industries called an official press conference. The event was simulcast live on national television and the Internet.

Questions and comments were fielded from a broad panel of curious experts, management gurus, and survivors of failed organizations.

"Can you guarantee that the Leadership Pill really works?" asked an analyst from the International Leadership Consortium.

"Of course," replied LPI's director of PR, who had earned her stripes in corporate communications. "Pre-trials with the Leadership Pill have been convincing enough for us to offer a money-back return policy," she said, smiling.

The CEO of the Workplace Affairs Bureau spoke up. "What is actually *in* this Leadership Pill?"

"What I can tell you is that the Leadership Pill contains extracts from the lessons of results-oriented leaders like Patton, Napoleon, and Attila the Hun," revealed the director of PR. "It's a powerful combination of ingredients."

Steve Cheney from the Association of Managers asked, "What is the recommended dosage for newly promoted supervisors? Are there any health risks, and is the Leadership Pill FDA approved?"

"Steve, the Leadership Pill is completely safe," replied the director of PR reassuringly. "It will be available over the counter or direct through LPI's website at leadership-pill.com."

Motioning to hold all questions for a moment, the director of PR pulled out a container of Leadership Pills from her briefcase.

"Now, if the cameras can zoom in for a close-up on the back of this pill bottle, our viewing audience will be able to see the dosage instructions. For those of you here today, please have a look at the flat-screen monitor to my left."

DOSAGE INSTRUCTIONS:

Take two Leadership Pills every six hours. Newly promoted leaders should double their dosage for the first 90 days.

If leadership ability is not improved, seek the advice of a human resources professional.

Taking the Leadership Pill with more than three caffeinated beverages per day may result in workaholism.

If recently laid off or have accepted an early retirement package, refrain from using this product to prevent passive-aggressive leadership behavior.

For more info, contact LPI at www.leadership-pill.com

The editor of the Leadership *Daily Voice,* taking scrupulous notes, finally posed the big question still on everyone's mind: "So how does it work? What happens when you actually take the Leadership Pill?"

"The Leadership Pill enhances your ability to lead," explained the director of PR. "When you take the Leadership Pill, you become more task-focused and action-oriented. Your ability to direct others and get results increases. Ultimately, the Leadership Pill works fast, putting you in control as a leader. There's nothing quite like it."

"That's amazing," remarked the editor.

"Indeed it is," agreed the director of PR. "But it's not a magical quick fix. According to the data we have collected, the Leadership Pill jump-starts the leadership center in your brain by stimulating its natural chemistry. Think of it this way: one dosage and the leadership lightbulb goes on. You get the job done in less time, take pleasure in meeting tight deadlines, and easily outperform the competition. Essentially, you become a leadership superhero."

"That *is* amazing!" echoed Bobbi Cassidy from the Leadership Assessment Association. "So how long does the effect of the Leadership Pill last?"

"That depends on the individual. We'll know a lot more as time goes on. One thing is for sure, though," said the director of PR as she paused for effect. "The Leadership Pill has the potential to become the first wonder drug for corporate America."

THE SURGE

The buzz following the press conference ignited a wave of new excitement about the Leadership Pill. Quantity orders flooded into LPI. Throughout every sector of industry, the initial interest in the Leadership Pill was overwhelming.

In just one week, the leadership-pill.com website received over seven million hits. Early statistics showed that the pill was already selling better than Viagra.

Shortly thereafter, Leadership Pill Industries unveiled its new slogan: *The Leadership Pill— When You've Got the Need to Lead*.

LPI's multitiered advertising campaign caught the attention of diverse audiences. Global distributors lined up to obtain Leadership Pill licensing rights. Industry consortiums were created in an effort to secure volume pricing.

Independent consultants, in a similar move, formed LPOs—Leadership Pill Organizations— to gain leveraging power. Mega-marketing conglomerates stepped forward to forge strategic partnerships with LPI.

The Leadership Pill caught on like wildfire. A national poll revealed that 87 percent of all managers favored the use of the Leadership Pill.

Even in government agencies, where skeptics had anticipated limited market penetration, the Leadership Pill was making a big splash.

Testimonials from satisfied customers were posted daily on the leadership-pill.com website:

"Looking back, I spent most of my time as a leader just trying to get by and survive. The Leadership Pill changed all of that. Now instead of reacting, I take initiative. I make decisions with confidence. Thanks, LPI."

> Jill—Minneapolis, Minnesota
> VP of Operations, Astor Pharmaceuticals

"I just got promoted to team leader and have hit the ground running. The Leadership Pill is a real lifesaver."

> Rob—New York City, New York
> Metro Service Team Leader, JLC Wireless

"It's hard to imagine life before the Leadership Pill. How did we ever get by without it?"

> Terry—Denver, Colorado
> Director of Sales, Powder Basin Ski Resort

Within months, Leadership Pill Industries went public and a professional management team was hired to oversee the landmark growth. Leadership-pill.com became a focal point not only for product sales but also for information on Leadership Pill videos, books on tape, and self-help publications.

The momentum was contagious. Leadership Pill product innovations hit the market in rapid succession: custom-colored pills, gel caplets, and even an extended dosage formula for busy leaders.

Cottage industries sprang up everywhere—Leadership Pill workshops, support groups, and advisory councils. Consultants seized the opportunity to make High Performance Pill initiatives a top priority for their clients. Soon Leadership Pill awareness programs were under way in virtually every major company.

Meanwhile, the founders of Leadership Pill Industries cashed in the majority of their stock options, as did dozens of LPI employees who had been there from the start. Wall Street pundits labeled them "pillionaires," while analysts questioned whether the heavy sell-off was an omen of things to come.

But sales of the Leadership Pill remained strong. For the moment, LPI's future looked brighter than ever.

THE CHALLENGE

As the popularity of the Leadership Pill soared, a front-page interview with the Effective Leader appeared in the *Leadership Times* and was picked up by nationally syndicated news wires. The Effective Leader, who had emerged as a staunch critic of the Leadership Pill, was convinced that the Leadership Pill was composed of the wrong ingredients.

"The problem with the Leadership Pill is what's in it. LPI tried to infuse their product with classic lessons in leadership, but apparently they extracted the wrong stuff," stated the Effective Leader. "I've observed people who use the Leadership Pill and find they are concerned only about getting results. Truly effective leaders also win the trust and respect of their team members. They excel at empowering others and letting them know that what they do is important."

The Effective Leader's comments sparked concern about the Leadership Pill and prompted a rush of inquiries at LPI corporate headquarters. In response to the growing chaos, the CEO of Leadership Pill Industries went to see his director of public relations.

"What's going on here?" demanded the CEO. "Give it to me in sixty seconds or less—I'm already late for my tee time."

"Bottom line, the Effective Leader insists that we've got a faulty pill. He's proposing a Pill-Free Challenge to prove it," explained the director of PR.

"Hold on a minute—the *Effective Leader*?" mused the CEO. "Is this guy for real?"

"The Effective Leader has been a respected business guru for decades. His view on leadership is summarized in this pill-shaped message that was printed in the interview," said the director of PR as she handed the CEO the article:

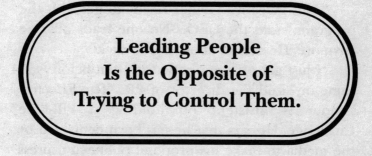

**Leading People
Is the Opposite of
Trying to Control Them.**

"This Effective Leader needs to get with the program," said the CEO. "No one leads pill-free anymore. He should know that by now."

"I just got off the phone with him before you came in," said the director of PR. "The Effective Leader is insistent on holding a Pill-Free Challenge. He says that he has been contacted by the media to make his proposal public at a press conference. The story will hit the papers the following day."

"Big deal. So tell me how the Pill-Free Challenge works, then," growled the CEO.

The director of PR paused for a moment. "It's kind of like a taste test: pill versus pill-free leadership. An independent panel selects two low-performing cross-functional teams that suffer from poor customer service, bad morale, and diminished profitability. The Effective Leader will step in as the leader of one team, with the goal of turning the team around over a twelve-month period without ever popping a Leadership Pill."

"What about the other team?" the CEO asked.

"The other team serves as the comparison group and is led by a current leader within that organization who must abstain from Leadership Pills until the start of the Pill-Free Challenge," the director of PR continued. "After that, this leader will take the Leadership Pill religiously over the course of the year while trying to turn the comparison group into a high-performing team."

"You must be joking," said the CEO with a snort. "The Effective Leader is doomed. Without Leadership Pills, he is sure to lose. This Pill-Free Challenge can become our advertisement for why the Pill is so essential to leadership survival. I'll get the marketing team on it right away. You notify this Effective Leader fellow that we accept his challenge. This is going to be a piece of cake."

And with that, the Pill-Free Challenge became official.

THE PREPARATION

The independent panel presiding over the Pill-Free Challenge scoured struggling companies and inefficient government agencies for several weeks. It was not difficult to find dysfunctional organizations given the reality of accelerated change, stiff competition, and ill-prepared leaders in every industry.

After careful deliberation, the panel identified two ailing companies that were far from profitable. The lowest performing individuals in these organizations were then selected as members of a newly formed cross-functional team within each company. These two groups would become the Pill-Free Challenge teams.

According to the independent panel's report, both teams were clearly in need of effective leadership. They had seen multiple management changes in the past two years. Team members were described in performance evaluations as lazy, disruptive, and apathetic. Their sense of customer service was marginal at best.

"Few individuals on these teams do more than the bare minimum to get by," explained the independent panel in their findings. "The majority of them would rather complain about unfair management practices than take responsibility for doing their jobs. It is clear that they perceive their chances of dying from heart failure to be greater than getting fired."

As the start of the Pill-Free Challenge drew near, members of the media from across the country swooped into town to position themselves for the start of the big event. Representatives from Leadership Pill Industries, including the CEO and the director of PR, were highly visible and on hand for meetings and interviews.

The Effective Leader also agreed to hold a brief question-and-answer session with the press on the eve of the Pill-Free Challenge. A large local meeting room was established for the conference, and soon enough it was filled with inquiring reporters.

"Why do you need a full year for the Pill-Free Challenge?" asked Geraldine Garcia, a noted national public radio commentator.

"It takes time to be truly effective when you are in charge of a team," said the Effective Leader.

"I see," she said, nodding. "So it's about having enough time to get results."

"Leading effectively means more than just getting results," responded the Effective Leader. "It means getting the commitment of the team. Many leaders focus only on the results part and forget about their people. They bang people over their heads until the job gets done. Their definition of success is the team's short-term output. The true test of leadership, on the other hand, is to win the trust and respect of the team, keep their motivation running high, and help them reach new heights. As a result, the team will work together and consistently perform well over time—even if the leader is not around."

The assembled reporters reflected on the Effective Leader's point as they read the pill-shaped button pinned to his lapel:

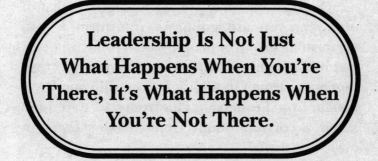

**Leadership Is Not Just
What Happens When You're
There, It's What Happens When
You're Not There.**

"So basically what you are telling us is that in one year you are going to transform a low-performing group of people whom you have never met into a highly productive and committed cross-functional team? In addition, you will completely abstain from Leadership Pills from start to finish?" asked a correspondent from *Worker's Digest* in obvious disbelief.

"Exactly," confirmed the Effective Leader.

"And what proof will we have that you are pill-free?" continued the correspondent.

"I'll be randomly drug tested, of course," reassured the Effective Leader.

"Aside from going without Leadership Pills," interjected a reporter, "how will the success or failure of your team's efforts in the Pill-Free Challenge be evaluated against that of the comparison group?"

"We will be using the Triple Bottom Line established by the independent panel to evaluate the progress of both teams on a quarterly basis," replied the Effective Leader.

"I'm not sure I understand," said the reporter. "What's the Triple Bottom Line?"

"The Triple Bottom Line is the way the judges will measure the three most important factors of performance," explained the Effective Leader. "It recognizes that great companies are the provider of choice, the employer of choice, and the investment of choice."

"It sounds like a lot of rhetoric to me," said the reporter. "Perhaps you could be more specific about how you plan to measure each part of the Triple Bottom Line."

"Of course. *Provider* of choice will be assessed by surveying our customers to find out how well their expectations were exceeded. When you turn customers into raving fans, they become part of your sales force. They want to brag about how well you treat them."

"I see," replied the reporter.

"*Employer* of choice, the next part of the Triple Bottom Line, will be measured by internal morale and work performance," the Effective Leader continued. "There is a powerful link between a gung ho motivated team and a team that consistently has solid productivity."

"This goes back to what you said before about how effective leaders get both commitment *and* results from their team," observed the reporter.

"Precisely. The remaining part of the Triple Bottom Line—*investor* of choice—is all about the financials. Profit needs to be weighted into the performance equation."

"All this stuff about raving fans and gung ho," interrupted a columnist from *The Business Insider.* "In the end, isn't it just the financials that are important?"

"I beg to differ," said the Effective Leader. "Let me leave you with a parting thought to consider." He pulled another pill-shaped button from his pocket and pinned it beside the other one on his lapel for the assembled group to read:

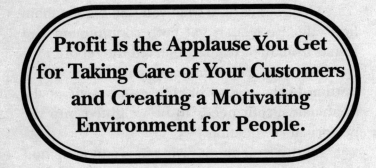

**Profit Is the Applause You Get
for Taking Care of Your Customers
and Creating a Motivating
Environment for People.**

The interview ended and the press crowd dispersed. Many of them were skeptical about the Effective Leader's chances of winning.

By the end of the evening, the odds on the street were 20 to 1 that the Effective Leader would try to sneak a few Leadership Pills before the Pill-Free Challenge was over. But in the morning the real story would begin to unfold.

THE SECRET BLEND

On the first day of the Pill-Free Challenge, the Effective Leader arrived promptly for the scheduled eight A.M. staff meeting with his new cross-functional team that had been selected by the independent panel. However, by eight-fifteen he was still the only one in the conference room.

Slowly people began to stroll in, most of them looking like they were half asleep. None of them greeted the Effective Leader. No one even smiled.

"Well, it is great to finally meet you all," remarked the Effective Leader. His words were met by blank stares and scowls.

"I am sure you all are curious to know a little bit more about this Pill-Free Challenge," continued the Effective Leader, ignoring the cold reception.

"Yeah, like how we got chosen for the wrong team," moaned Javier Robles, the human resources generalist. "With you being pill-free while our opponents' leader is juiced up on Leadership Pills, we don't stand a chance. Twelve months from now, we'll all be looking for work but nobody will hire us. We'll be called 'pill-free losers' for the rest of our lives."

"Well, Javier," responded the Effective Leader as he eyed Javier's name tag, "I have yet to meet a group of people who are incapable of becoming a high-performing, committed team since I learned about the Secret Blend for effective leadership."

"The *Secret Blend*? It sounds like a new concoction at Starbucks." Javier laughed. "What are you going to do, dry-roast us into submission?"

"I sure hope not," said the Effective Leader, grinning, "though I *do* plan to make the three ingredients of the Secret Blend the foundation of how we operate as a team."

"So enough with the suspense and coffee metaphors. Just give us the specifics of the Secret Blend," said Mary Weisman from business operations, already growing impatient. She had worked at the company longer than anyone in the room.

"With all due respect, Mary, simply *telling* you is not the best way to learn. Frankly, I made a lot of mistakes as a leader and got plenty of education at the School of Hard Knocks before I discovered the beauty of the Secret Blend. The best way to get a handle on it is for you to start with your own definition of leadership," said the Effective Leader as he pointed to the question written on the whiteboard behind him: **"If you could have anything you wanted in a leader, what would you wish for?"**

The room fell silent. Several minutes went by until Denzel Frederick, the lead sales rep, spoke up. "What would I wish for in a leader? How about a leader who could permanently disappear!"

Everyone cringed. The Effective Leader took the wisecrack in stride. "If you were a genie, Denzel, I guess I would be in trouble. How about giving it another shot?" he suggested.

"Okay," said Denzel, realizing that his attempt to ruffle the Effective Leader had failed. "I wish that leaders would just tell us the truth. You know, honesty instead of lies."

"I appreciate your candor," praised the Effective Leader. "Now can you give me an example?"

"*I* can," inserted Daniel Noonan, who was in the process of polishing up his résumé. "It's when top management tells us there won't be any layoffs and then three weeks later half of my project team is collecting unemployment."

"You've got *that* right," said Li Young Kitoko, a software engineer. She had intentionally pursued a nonmanagement IT track due to her disillusionment with the organizational power structure. "I'd trust a politician before I'd trust a manager."

"What I hear you all saying is that you want leaders to give you the straight scoop," summarized the Effective Leader. "You want them to walk their talk."

"Yes, I want leaders to do what they say they are going to do," Li Young agreed.

"All the surveys show that the number one thing people want in a leader is integrity," continued the Effective Leader. "Integrity is about creating a set of operating values and then living true to them. When a leader's actions embody the organization's values, the result is a value-driven culture. *This* is the essence of **integrity**—the first ingredient of the Secret Blend."

The Effective Leader proceeded to write a new message on the whiteboard:

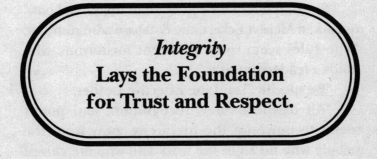

Integrity
**Lays the Foundation
for Trust and Respect.**

"I wish it felt like we were all in the same boat," remarked Melissa Eckert, the database administrator. "The rules seem to be different for anyone who holds a leadership title."

"Be specific," said the Effective Leader.

"All of the money, recognition, and power seems to move up the hierarchy, away from the people who do all of the work and who are closest to the customer," explained Melissa. "That's not what I call being in the same boat."

"It's a sense of being disconnected. Each of us plays a role in the problem," observed Larry Jensen from marketing. "We are so concerned about pushing our own agendas and protecting our own turf that we forget we are on the same team."

"Sometimes it is easy to get self-absorbed and territorial, Larry," noted the Effective Leader. "The second ingredient of the Secret Blend—**partnership** —implies that leaders need to help their people work, learn, and grow together in unity." On the whiteboard he then recorded:

Partnership
**Harvests the Potential
of the Team.**

"What else would you wish for in a leader?" asked the Effective Leader.

"I'd like leaders to get to know us for who we are," answered Sarah Hawkins, who worked in accounts receivable.

"That is on my wish list too," said Ryan Fletcher, a seasoned customer service agent. "The only time my last boss spoke to me was when something went wrong. I don't think he even knew my name."

"Good leaders get to know people beyond their job titles," pointed out the Effective Leader. "They find out what makes each individual on their team unique."

"Sorry, guys, but the warm fuzzy thing is where I draw the line," said the production supervisor, Mo Zellinger, looking disgusted.

"Why?" asked the Effective Leader. "Don't you like to know that you are appreciated?"

"I still have to do my job whether I feel appreciated or not," Mo responded. "I don't get paid to be happy."

"Your apathy seems to fit with the culture around here, Mo," observed the Effective Leader.

"So what is your point?" insisted Mo.

"My point," said the Effective Leader, "is that it does not seem like most of you are complaining about getting thanked too much. **Affirmation—** the final ingredient of the Secret Blend for effective leadership—makes people feel valued."

The Effective Leader once more directed the team's attention to the whiteboard:

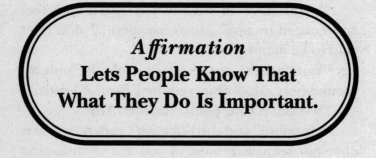

Affirmation
**Lets People Know That
What They Do Is Important.**

The Effective Leader paused for a moment, surveying the faces of each team member. Then he asked, "If I could fulfill your wishes for what you have said you want in a leader—integrity, partnership, and affirmation—do you believe that together we can become a high-performing team and win this Pill-Free Challenge?"

Several team members nodded their heads. Others seemed noncommittal, simply waiting for the Effective Leader to continue.

"Between now and our next staff meeting, I want you to reflect on what our mutual roles will be in making these three ingredients of the Secret Blend come to life," the Effective Leader said. "I hope to see you all on time at the next staff meeting."

As the group left the room, the Effective Leader noticed that while some team members seemed more alive and energetic than before, others clearly were not buying into the task at hand. *And so the fun begins,* the Effective Leader thought to himself.

THE SEARCH FOR INTEGRITY

Later that week the Effective Leader underwent his first round of drug testing and the results were released to Leadership Pill Industries and the media. Word quickly spread that he was pill-free and making progress with his team. However, there were already early indications that the Pill-Free Challenge comparison group was achieving sizable gains on each of the Triple Bottom Line metrics. By contrast, the Effective Leader's team was off to a slow start.

On the morning of his next staff meeting, the Effective Leader was greeted by a couple of team members as he entered the conference room at seven-fifty A.M.

"We wanted to get a good seat," they explained. By eight o'clock, more than half of the team was present and seated.

"Thanks for showing up," said the Effective Leader. "That's always a good sign. Now where did we leave off?"

"What about the others?" Denzel Frederick cut in.

"We can start without them," replied the Effective Leader.

"I thought you were all about being a team," said Denzel.

"I am," the Effective Leader answered. "But high-performing teams cannot slow down for those who fail to live up to their commitments. We all agreed to be here this morning. People who don't do what they say they are going to do are showing a lack of respect for the rest of us. Their integrity is essentially at stake."

"It sounds like we're back to the Secret Blend," said Melissa Eckert.

"Yes, the Secret Blend definitely applies here," agreed the Effective Leader. "In fact, the first step in moving toward a culture of integrity is to build an infrastructure of trust and respect. Let's talk about ways that both you and I can make this happen through effective leadership."

"I thought leading was *your* job," said Melissa.

"That is true. But I can't be effective unless each of you does your part from a self-leadership perspective. It's a two-way street," pointed out the Effective Leader as he turned to the whiteboard.

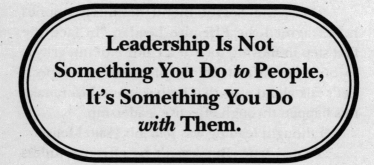

**Leadership Is Not
Something You Do *to* People,
It's Something You Do
with Them.**

"You mentioned the key to integrity is trust and respect," said Sarah Hawkins. "Aren't they the same thing?"

"Not really," replied the Effective Leader. "Let's start with respect. If I respect you, I face you. This means that I want to involve you in decision making and hear your opinions. It's why leadership is something we do together. In a low-respect environment, though, I don't care what you think. If I don't respect you, I have my back to you."

"That sounds like every leader we've had in the past," recalled Sarah.

"Unfortunately, some leaders think that *they* are the inventors of all good things," observed the Effective Leader. "They act like they could care less about what other people think."

"Respect goes both ways though, doesn't it?" asked Li Young Kitoko.

"Absolutely. For instance, I hope you'll listen to me just as I want to listen to you," said the Effective Leader.

"I've got an idea of how to make respect a reality around here," Daniel Noonan announced as Mo Zellinger, Mary Weisman, and Javier Robles straggled in.

"Let's hear it," urged the Effective Leader.

"Uphold the Golden Rule—do unto others as you want them to do unto you," continued Daniel. "As project manager, I want my opinions to be respected. Thus, I need to respect the opinions of others."

"Leading by example is another way to put respect into action," added Ryan Fletcher. "The way I speak to customers sets the tone for how they view me and our company. My behavior directly impacts their level of respect."

"You are right on track," said the Effective Leader as he turned and wrote on the whiteboard:

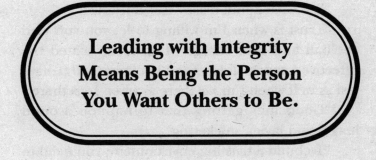

**Leading with Integrity
Means Being the Person
You Want Others to Be.**

"But what about trust?" asked Ryan.

"Trust is when I'm willing to let you run with the ball and take charge of an area," stated the Effective Leader. "It is when I know you will behave just as well when I'm *not* there as when I *am* there."

"Good luck getting that to happen around here," said Javier, snickering.

"To build a trusting environment, you need to have a set of operating values that guide people's behaviors when they are working on organizational goals," responded the Effective Leader, disregarding Javier's cynicism.

"I imagine you would like our three values to be integrity, partnership, and affirmation," Denzel Frederick said with a smirk.

"Well, what do *you* think?" asked the Effective Leader.

"If we are going to work together as a team, then I guess these values make sense," Denzel conceded.

"The importance of living true to our Secret Blend values will become even clearer as we learn more about them," assured the Effective Leader.

"You take this stuff pretty seriously," said Mary Weisman.

"We all should. I've seen companies that put their values on plaques and banners that hang on the walls, but everyone thinks they are a joke. No one uses these values to make decisions and leaders fail to hold people accountable for not behaving in accordance with them," explained the Effective Leader. "This disregard for the organization's values leads to a breakdown in trust." He again turned to the whiteboard and wrote:

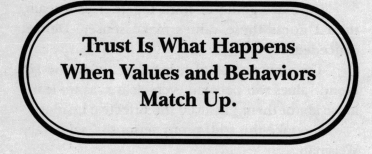

**Trust Is What Happens
When Values and Behaviors
Match Up.**

"So how do we get started on building trust and respect around here?" asked Melissa Eckert.

"First, I'd like you to make a list of the top three things you really like about working here and the top three things that you really dislike," said the Effective Leader.

The team had no trouble making their lists. In debriefing the exercise, the Effective Leader had members of the group share their findings. "Interesting work" was cited as the biggest positive, followed by "decent pay" and "pleasant working conditions." "Broken promises" led the list of negatives, with "no team spirit" and "low recognition for accomplishments" close behind.

"Why not just focus on the good news?" asked Li Young Kitoko.

"We need to know what isn't working so that we can identify where to start making improvements. A key aspect of having integrity is that we trust each other enough to share our shortcomings as well as our strengths. When we know we won't be beaten up for our deficiencies, we can work on finding ways to improve them," said the Effective Leader.

As the team members continued working on ways to build respect and trust, the connection between the Secret Blend value of integrity and their ability to work effectively as a team became obvious.

They strived to win the respect of their coworkers, customers, and the Effective Leader by actively listening and taking the initiative to help out. In subsequent staff meetings, they took inventory not only of where they had been successful, but where they had fallen short of the mark. Gradually a sense of trust grew among team members and between them and the Effective Leader. He too was doing his part to enrich the evolving culture of integrity.

In the next staff meeting, the Effective Leader noted, "Many managers pontificate about having an open door policy when the door is in effect bolted shut. If they aren't hiding in their offices or taking a three-hour lunch, the frowns on their faces say 'do not enter.' People never know how to get hold of them."

"That's a perfect description of the leaders who came before you," remarked Mo Zellinger. "But how do we know you won't just live up to their legacy?"

"Leaders who live up to the promise of being truly accessible to their constituents do so by taking out all of the guesswork, Mo. They show their integrity by behaving in alignment with the same values to which they hold their own teams accountable. This underscores the importance of why you and I need to consistently live up to the Secret Blend values," the Effective Leader pointed out as he put a new message on the whiteboard:

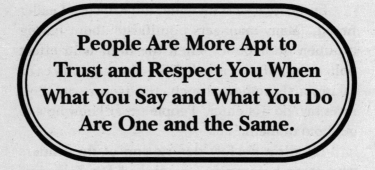

People Are More Apt to Trust and Respect You When What You Say and What You Do Are One and the Same.

The Effective Leader then unveiled a scheduling system for booking time with him online. He also instituted what he called a No-Meeting Mondays policy.

"Going forward, you will have direct access to my schedule. Notice that I am not scheduling any outside meetings or conference calls on Mondays," said the Effective Leader. "This will ensure that I have at least one full day each week dedicated to one-on-one coaching sessions and informal quality time with you. As we continue to work together— and you trust me and I trust you—I probably won't have to put that much time aside."

The team was thrilled to see the Effective Leader walking his talk as a reflection of his commitment to the Secret Blend value of integrity. However, they were still a bit hesitant to completely trust him as the first quarter of the Pill-Free Challenge drew to a close.

THE PARTNERSHIP IMPERATIVE

The results for the first quarter of the Pill-Free Challenge were published in a press release issued by the independent panel of evaluators. While the Effective Leader's team had made steady progress in building integrity, their Triple Bottom Line was not improving as quickly as that of the comparison group.

"We have a healthy foundation for growth," the Effective Leader told reporters. "It would be unrealistic to think that we could go from being a dysfunctional team to a high-performing one in only ninety days. Don't give up on us yet."

The Pill-Free Challenge comparison group, on the other hand, showed significant gains in all three performance areas of the Triple Bottom Line. The leader of this team, who was on a steady regiment of Leadership Pills as planned, was hailed for being decisive, forceful, and confident.

"Let the world bear witness to the strength of the Leadership Pill," boasted LPI's CEO in a televised interview. "Customer service, morale, and productivity are getting better day by day. Profitability is improving too. This is one potent pill!"

LPI's stock climbed on the favorable news. The front page of every major paper heralded the success of the Leadership Pill in the headlines. Popular print journals featured cover stories on the Leadership Pill with sexy captions such as "Pill of the Century," "A Leader's Little Helper," and "The Safest Drug in America."

The Effective Leader was not intimidated by the comparison group's commanding lead, nor that they had raced out of the starting gate and stayed in front. His first action at the outset of the second quarter of the Pill-Free Challenge was to pay a late-night visit to his team's production facility.

"What brings you to the graveyard shift?" asked the shop steward. "Did somebody forget to clock in?"

"Don't worry, I don't bite," promised the Effective Leader.

"Then why the unexpected visit?" demanded the shop steward.

"I wanted to see if I could lend a hand this evening. I haven't had a chance to meet you all yet and I thought this would be a great way to introduce myself," replied the Effective Leader.

"You must be a glutton for punishment," insisted the shop steward.

"You may be right," said the Effective Leader. "But I am used to rolling up my sleeves."

They bantered a while and then the Effective Leader got busy. At the end of the shift, the shop steward pulled him aside and remarked, "This is a big step toward forging a better partnership between labor and management. Tonight you've shown all of us that you value what we do."

The Effective Leader stuck around for coffee and Krispy Kreme doughnuts with the crew. After what seemed like an endless series of high fives, he said goodbye and drove home at dawn for a well-deserved rest.

Later that day, the Effective Leader returned for a staff meeting. He wrote the following message on the whiteboard:

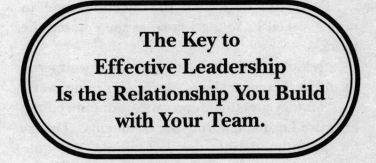

**The Key to
Effective Leadership
Is the Relationship You Build
with Your Team.**

"Why did he switch the meeting time to noon?" asked Li Young Kitoko as she entered the room.

"It looks like he had a tough night," whispered Ryan Fletcher, chuckling. "Maybe he's hung over."

"Midday greetings, everyone," announced the Effective Leader, ignoring the comments. "Thanks for accommodating the last-minute schedule change. I had a fruitful visit last night with the graveyard shift."

"You did?" Ryan gasped in surprise. "No manager has ever gone to see them."

"You should try it yourself some time. I am sure they would appreciate it," said the Effective Leader. "Sometimes it's easy to forget that we are all in this together."

"So what's the game plan for today?" asked Larry Jensen. "I'm getting hungry."

"Don't worry, we will eat," replied the Effective Leader.

"Great," said Larry. "Are you taking us out somewhere nice?"

"Sorry, Larry, not this time," said the Effective Leader with a smile. "I'm having food brought in."

"Sounds like a working lunch," groaned Mary Weisman.

"I would prefer to call it a lunch-and-learn session. There is some interesting stuff I want to go over with you today."

For the next half hour, the Effective Leader discussed the big picture of where the organization was headed. He gave the team a preview of the revised budget and revenue forecast, then handed them a copy of the last quarterly report.

"Wow!" exclaimed Daniel Noonan as he and his team members thumbed through the numbers. "I've never seen any of this before."

"Now I understand why we are so backed up in accounts receivable," said Sarah Hawkins. "Just look at all of these overdue accounts."

"Think about how much uncollected money we have sitting out there," remarked Mo Zellinger. "No wonder our profit is so far under goal."

"Most managers never expose their staffs to this level of company reporting," observed the Effective Leader. "They act like it is top-secret information. Essentially, it is the opposite of working in partnership. People run around in the dark shooting for targets they can't even see."

"I know the feeling," said Javier Robles. "I'm responsible for filling open jobs, but I don't learn how many people have left the company until thirty days after they are already out the door."

"Our last boss thought we were too dumb to understand the numbers," added Denzel Frederick.

"If you can balance your checkbook, you can read a management report," replied the Effective Leader. "Our second Secret Blend value is rooted in sharing this kind of information. Essentially, partnership epitomizes the two-way street: both you and I feel the gain and the pain. After all, I don't want to be the only one losing sleep at night!"

As lunch arrived, the Effective Leader wrote this note on the whiteboard:

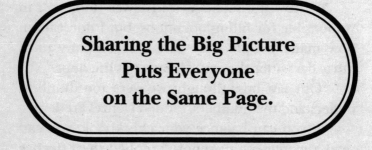

**Sharing the Big Picture
Puts Everyone
on the Same Page.**

The group continued to discuss these ideas over lunch and then finally cleared their plates.

"Let me ask one other thing of you before we close our lunch meeting," said the Effective Leader. "As you know, I have set aside Mondays for the sole purpose of spending quality, constructive time with you. What I would like to do is set up weekly one-on-one sessions in increments of fifteen to thirty minutes."

"I don't get it. Why are you doing this?" asked Mary Weisman.

"Scheduling one-on-ones ensures that I am free to meet with each of you on a regular basis," replied the Effective Leader. "In other words, I want to talk to you about your concerns and how I can help. I want to discuss *your* agendas. It's your time to be heard by me. Ultimately, I want you to know that I'm not just here to evaluate your performance. I want to work in partnership with you to help you win. And when you win, I win."

"Sounds like a winning proposition to me." Melissa Eckert smiled.

The lunch-and-learn sessions flourished over the next three months. Larry Jensen and Sarah Hawkins took it upon themselves to hold their own variations on the theme for coworkers who wanted to learn more about marketing and financial accounting. To their delight, the events were well attended.

As the weeks passed, the Effective Leader continued to test negative for Leadership Pill usage. Throughout the second quarter of the Pill-Free Challenge, he developed additional ways to build partnership through shared learning. First, he piloted a peer-mentoring project where senior members of the staff helped acclimate new hires to the company as they came on board. Then he began bringing team members with him to meetings he had previously attended alone.

"I want to put you in the thick of the action so that you can get solid experience and learn," explained the Effective Leader.

He also followed through on holding one-on-one meetings with each of his people. In the beginning, they were a little guarded with respect to sharing their concerns and needs. But when the Effective Leader didn't punish them—even when they shared some bad news—they began to trust the process. This regimen of weekly continuous learning created a steady two-way flow of information and helped the Effective Leader's transition from simply directing his people to becoming more of a coach.

In addition, the Effective Leader fostered a culture of partnership by establishing a collaborative learning process that included cross-training and job rotations. As the initiative took hold, new career paths evolved and the collective skill sets of the team expanded.

The last thing the Effective Leader launched in the second quarter of the Pill-Free Challenge was a leadership shadowing program for interested team members. Melissa Eckert was the first volunteer.

"I would like you to run next week's staff meeting," the Effective Leader told her when she signed up. "It is the last meeting of the quarter."

"I don't get it, are you headed out of town or something?" asked Melissa.

"No, I just thought that you might like to give it a shot," responded the Effective Leader. "Too many managers think that they are the only ones capable of conducting a meeting. Meetings take up a lot of my time, so it makes sense to have others share the load. Besides, group facilitation is a valuable skill to have."

"I'll give it a try, but I don't know the first thing about getting up in front of people," Melissa confessed.

"I'll teach you," promised the Effective Leader. "The goal is to have you meet with success, not fall on your face."

Melissa met with the Effective Leader several times that week to work on improving her skills.

"You'll do fine," said the Effective Leader. "Don't worry if you feel a little nervous."

On the morning of the staff meeting, every team member was in the room by eight o'clock— an unprecedented event for the team. "At least *that* is a good sign," Melissa sighed. She glanced over at the Effective Leader one last time. His confident gaze put her at ease as she welcomed the group.

Once Melissa got started, she did not look back. It was quickly apparent that she was more prepared than they could have guessed. In closing, Melissa used the whiteboard to share what she had learned about partnership that week:

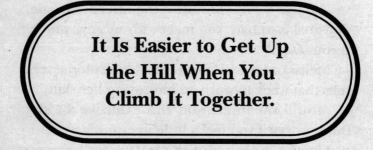

**It Is Easier to Get Up
the Hill When You
Climb It Together.**

In the days that followed, the team took Melissa's message to heart. "Climbing the hill together" extended beyond just working in partnership with the Effective Leader, they determined. It meant building a stronger sense of partnership with each other as well. In the final analysis, they knew they needed to be more mutually supportive and willing to help one another.

Melissa took the first step by offering her time to anyone on the team who wanted to learn how to run an effective meeting. Li Young Kitoko took the initiative to work on debugging the human resources information system software that had been preventing Javier Robles from getting real-time hiring statistics and job requisition data. Gradually, the examples grew and a team culture of caring and reciprocity began to emerge.

THE ART OF AFFIRMATION

The second quarter results of the Pill-Free Challenge were submitted to the press. As in the previous quarter, the comparison group showed better performance on customer satisfaction and profit. But their morale scores began to show a downward trend. In contrast, the Effective Leader's team demonstrated some real gains on each of the Triple Bottom Line indicators.

"We are making solid progress in becoming the provider of choice, the employer of choice, and the investment of choice," commented the Effective Leader. "The game is far from over, and we are going to win it without the Leadership Pill."

The Effective Leader was determined to capitalize on his team's progress. At the next staff meeting, he reviewed the second-quarter Pill-Free Challenge results with his team.

"Thanks for your efforts. While we still have a long way to go, we are doing a much better job with integrity and partnership. Now we need to find ways to keep it going so that we can maximize our Triple Bottom Line. This is where the third Secret Blend value—affirmation—comes into play."

"How do we put affirmation into action?" asked Daniel Noonan.

"Saying thank you is one simple way. You can make a huge difference in the way others feel about themselves by letting them know that you appreciate their efforts and recognize that what they do is important," said the Effective Leader. "The key is to follow the rules of effective praising."

"The rules?" responded Daniel.

"Yes," replied the Effective Leader. "Praise is most effective when it is specific, sincere, and given as soon as possible after desired behavior occurs. It should be consistently applied only to situations where praise is warranted, but not given every single time a person does something right."

"I followed you all the way until that last part about not praising every time," said Daniel.

"Think about it this way, Danny," explained the Effective Leader. "Not praising people every time they do something right helps them learn to praise themselves instead of relying on others to do it all the time."

"That makes a lot of sense," agreed Daniel.

The next day, the Effective Leader gave Mo Zellinger a call. "I want to speak to you right after lunch," he said. "The sooner the better."

Mo anxiously called a couple of coworkers to see if they knew what was going on.

"Probably layoffs," Mary Weisman warned.

"It was nice knowing you," responded Javier Robles.

The Effective Leader asked Mo if he wanted a cup of coffee when he arrived.

"No, thanks, let's just get this over with," said Mo.

"Do you know why you are here today?" asked the Effective Leader.

Mo's mind raced with negative thoughts. He knew he must have done something wrong.

"I want to take a moment to let you know how pleased I am with your work lately," continued the Effective Leader. "Production numbers are up and payroll is under budget. Thanks for your positive attitude and effort."

Mo's jaw dropped. He was speechless.

"You look like you've seen a ghost," said the Effective Leader. "What's wrong?"

"I thought you called me in here to lay me off," Mo answered.

"Why is it that people think they are in trouble every time they hear from their boss?" asked the Effective Leader. "I wanted to compliment you, not downsize you."

Mo suddenly realized that he had earned the trust and respect of the Effective Leader—and that the Effective Leader had earned his as well. He reflected on the power of praising, how it was an easy, cost-free way to make people feel valued. Later that day, the Effective Leader sent a note to everyone on the team:

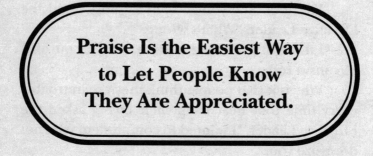

**Praise Is the Easiest Way
to Let People Know
They Are Appreciated.**

Upon reading the Effective Leader's latest message, Denzel Frederick had an idea about how to create a two-way street for affirmation. On his own initiative, he instituted a grass-roots program called "Here's a Salute to You."

"When I catch a team member making integrity, partnership, or affirmation a reality, I award them on the spot with a personally signed certificate that thanks them for being a Secret Blend Ambassador —or what I call an SBA," Denzel explained with enthusiasm.

Other team members soon adopted Denzel's idea. Larry Jensen even started giving out certificates to external customers and vendors who exemplified SBA behavior.

The Effective Leader, who firmly believed in the concept of catching people doing things right, had a supply of "Here's a Salute to You" certificates printed up for every team member. He inscribed this note on the cover of each pad:

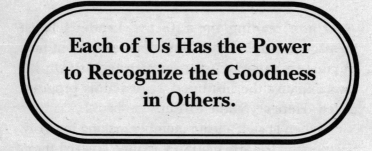

Each of Us Has the Power to Recognize the Goodness in Others.

The Effective Leader's team found that there were endless opportunities to award "Here's a Salute to You" certificates to deserving Secret Blend Ambassadors. However, there were also times when things did not go as well. When team members performed at a substandard level, it was clearly not appropriate to praise them.

The Effective Leader knew that under-performing individuals were still capable of doing a good job. Instead of focusing his energy on their poor performance, he redirected their behaviors to get them back on track. To do this, he sat down with them to establish revised game plans, assigned them to projects where their talents could be better utilized, or enlisted their fellow team members to serve as mentors. The Effective Leader then affirmed these individuals with praise when their performance improved.

In the spirit of affirmation, the Effective Leader also decided to pilot family-friendly scheduling alternatives such as flextime, job sharing, telecommuting, and compressed workweeks.

"I made the bold assumption that you all had a life outside of work," he told the team.

In addition, the Effective Leader instituted mental hygiene stress relief breaks as affirmations of stellar performance. Examples included paid time off, gift certificates for massages, fun in the workplace projects, team building initiatives, and complimentary gym memberships.

"A mental hygiene break is when you take a hiatus from work to refresh your mind," he pointed out. "It is a conscious time-out for your brain."

The Effective Leader emailed the following message to each team member that week:

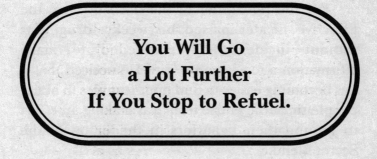

**You Will Go
a Lot Further
If You Stop to Refuel.**

For the remainder of the third quarter, the Effective Leader passed his weekly drug tests without incident and proceeded to make affirmation a top team priority. He noticed that it was becoming easier to find opportunities to praise people since the entire team was making an effort to ground their behaviors in the values of the Secret Blend.

Meanwhile, rumors about declining morale in the Pill-Free Challenge comparison group began to circulate. Several unconfirmed reports cited that the leader of the comparison group had grown accustomed to using an authoritarian and often relentless "my way or the highway" leadership approach. While this coercive style had initially impressed the team as being forceful and decisive, they now felt battered and demoralized.

Another account alleged that the productivity of the Pill-Free Challenge comparison group was steadily decreasing and that the team's leader had become even more overbearing and controlling. In order to get results, people were being overworked to the point of burnout.

LPI's director of PR responded to the media in hopes of quelling stockholder fears. "It is no coincidence that for two quarters in a row, the undisputed front-runner in the Pill-Free Challenge is the group whose leader is taking daily doses of the Leadership Pill," she remarked. "Needless to say, we are quite pleased with the results."

In spite of the director of PR's confident rhetoric, the National Council for Pill Safety launched an investigative probe to examine the long-term effects of using the Leadership Pill. LPI's stock dropped for the first time ever as the third quarter of the Pill-Free Challenge came to an abrupt close.

PERFECTING THE BLEND

"It's a Race to the Finish!" read newspaper headlines from across the country after the Pill-Free Challenge third quarter results were announced.

To the shock of the business press who were following the event, the Effective Leader's team was now neck and neck with the comparison group on profit, but was pulling ahead on morale and customer service.

"Our Triple Bottom Line is looking better than ever," stated the Effective Leader. "Customer complaints are way down and morale and operational performance are close to outstanding. While our profit margin is just slightly under goal, we plan to make a big push over these last three months of the Pill-Free Challenge."

LPI's CEO did not respond to reporters' questions when asked why he thought the Pill-Free Challenge comparison group's numbers had fallen from the previous quarter. He also declined to comment on speculation that while the Leadership Pill was able to produce quick short-term results, it might not be as effective in the long run.

Perhaps the most shocking finding was the increase in turnover among employees in the Pill-Free Challenge comparison group. Exit interviews by members of the press suggested that the leader of this group never seemed willing to share power and information with the team. This kept team members in a state of dependency that made them feel subordinate, unmotivated, and resentful.

LPI stock plummeted as Leadership Pill consumer confidence eroded. Hoping to fend off a fourth quarter disaster, the leader of the comparison group began taking quadruple dosages of the Leadership Pill.

Amidst all of the chaos, the Effective Leader kept his team focused on the three Secret Blend values.

"It is time to rally," he told the team in their staff meeting. "This is the home stretch, so don't hold back."

"What is our plan of attack?" asked Sarah Hawkins eagerly.

"I am delegating the responsibility for making that decision to the team," responded the Effective Leader. "Throughout the year, you have gained competence and confidence in putting integrity, partnership, and affirmation to work. So for the remainder of the Pill-Free Challenge, how you make integrity, partnership, and affirmation come to life is your call."

"And if we fail?" asked Javier Robles.

"A wise leader once told me to draw the target and get out of the way," said the Effective Leader.

"I don't get it," said Javier.

"Have confidence in your ability to think for yourselves. Don't check your brains at the door. I am empowering you to get to the goal however you see fit. Just use your best judgment and I will be here to back you up," assured the Effective Leader as he wrote a new message on the whiteboard:

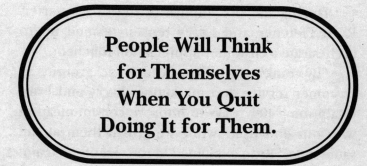

**People Will Think
for Themselves
When You Quit
Doing It for Them.**

During the first month of the final quarter, Ryan Fletcher and Larry Jensen teamed up to orchestrate a customer appreciation luncheon.

"By combining our respective backgrounds in customer service and marketing, Larry and I are establishing new ways to improve communication with our end users while we affirm them at the same time," Ryan explained to the rest of the team.

"Strengthening the connection with our customers builds mutual trust and partnership," Larry added.

Meanwhile, Melissa Eckert completed her leadership shadowing program and then leveraged Li Young Kitoko's software development expertise to construct a computer-based leadership skills train-the-trainer. Prior to beta testing, they brought the Effective Leader a prototype.

"We named the program appropriately— 'Leadership: It's More Than a Pill.' We also came up with a fitting message to kick off the first module," Melissa told the Effective Leader as she clicked on the appropriate screen:

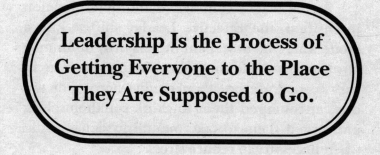

Leadership Is the Process of Getting Everyone to the Place They Are Supposed to Go.

As the team's confidence and determination intensified, the Effective Leader shifted into a mode where he now spent the majority of his time ensuring that team members had the resources they needed. He gave them credit where credit was due, encouraged them to think for themselves, and urged them to take mental hygiene breaks when necessary to reduce stress.

The Effective Leader also continued to make himself readily accessible to team members through the one-on-one coaching process and spent time in the trenches actively soliciting their ideas for ongoing improvement. As the end of the Pill-Free Challenge drew near, it was clear to him that each member of the team was living the Secret Blend values.

"No question about it, *this* is a high-performing team," the Effective Leader declared at the last staff meeting.

Melissa Eckert, on her own initiative, led the team through the meeting agenda. Her facilitation skills had noticeably improved.

Upon Melissa's closing remarks, Denzel Frederick stood up and presented the Effective Leader with a giant "Here's a Salute to You" certificate signed by every team member.

"We realize that Secret Blend Ambassadorship is a two-way street. This is our way of affirming you for everything you have taught us about the Secret Blend," said Denzel. "You are the ultimate SBA!"

Touched by the team's gesture, the Effective Leader left the team with a final thought on the whiteboard:

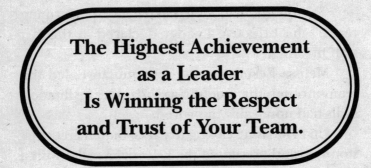

**The Highest Achievement
as a Leader
Is Winning the Respect
and Trust of Your Team.**

THE END AND A BEGINNING

A large crowd had gathered at the press conference where the independent panel of evaluators prepared to declare the final results of the Pill-Free Challenge. After the audience settled into their seats, the panel spokesperson read the official statement to the media:

"After twelve months of exciting competition, we are honored to announce that the winner of the Pill-Free Challenge is in fact the team that was led for a full year without Leadership Pills. We would like to formally congratulate the Effective Leader and his top-notch team."

The Effective Leader's staff stood up to cheer and applaud as he got up on the podium to address the room.

"We have exceeded the people and performance goals on our Triple Bottom Line," the Effective Leader began. "I am grateful to this talented group of individuals who deserve the credit for making this happen. While it is indeed a remarkable accomplishment, I knew all along that we could do it."

The Effective Leader paused to shake the hand of each team member. Then he turned his attention toward the crowd.

"Effective leaders earn the respect and trust of their team on a daily basis," he pointed out. "They realize it takes time to perfect the right blend of integrity, partnership, and affirmation. In essence, the Secret Blend is a potent pill for effective leadership over the long haul."

The Effective Leader looked over to his team again with obvious pride and gratitude. Then he continued, "The team and I want you all to have a take-away of the precious nuggets of leadership wisdom that guided us throughout the Pill-Free Challenge. These simple truths are what helped us live true to the values we adopted from the Secret Blend. They can be applied right away by anyone who wants to be a more effective team leader and self-leader."

The Effective Leader then pulled out a stack of laminated handouts that he had the team distribute to the crowd as he read aloud from his own copy.

THE SECRET BLEND
FOR EFFECTIVE LEADERSHIP

Leadership Is Not Something You Do *to* People,
It's Something You Do *with* Them

INTEGRITY

- Leading with Integrity Means Being the Person You Want Others to Be.
- Trust Is What Happens When Values and Behaviors Match Up.
- People Are More Apt to Trust and Respect You When What You Say and What You Do Are One and the Same.

PARTNERSHIP

- The Key to Effective Leadership Is the Relationship You Build with Your Team.
- Sharing the Big Picture Puts Everyone on the Same Page.
- It Is Easier to Get Up the Hill When You Climb It Together.

AFFIRMATION

- Praise Is the Easiest Way to Let People Know They Are Appreciated.
- Each of Us Has the Power to Recognize the Goodness in Others.
- You Will Go a Lot Further If You Stop to Refuel.

PERFECTING THE BLEND

- People Will Think for Themselves When You Quit Doing It for Them.
- Leadership Is the Process of Getting Everyone to the Place They Are Supposed to Go.
- The Highest Achievement As a Leader Is Winning the Respect and Trust of Your Team.

The Effective Leader received a standing ovation as he stepped down from the stage to join his team in celebrating their achievement. At that moment, the Effective Leader was struck by the powerful realization that this group of individuals had done more than win the Pill-Free Challenge. They now were capable of living the core values of integrity, partnership, and affirmation without him.

This is what effective leadership is all about, the Effective Leader thought to himself as he said his good-byes.

Meanwhile, the director of Pubic Relations from Leadership Pill Industries—still shocked by the outcome of the Pill-Free Challenge—had not moved from her chair. "The Leadership Pill is dead," she muttered with a scowl to LPI's CEO, who was seated beside her.

"Nonsense!" said the CEO with surprising enthusiasm. "Let's give the Leadership Pill new life."

"I don't get it," said the director of PR.

"Now that the Secret Blend for effective leadership is not a secret anymore, we simply need to reformulate the Leadership Pill," replied the CEO. "Just like the Effective Leader said, integrity, partnership, and affirmation are the ingredients for leadership over the long haul."

The director of PR regained her composure. "You've got a point there," she said to the CEO as they began a wild brainstorming session. "Maybe we could recruit the Effective Leader to be on our research and development team. We could change our slogan to *Leadership for a Lifetime....*"

ACKNOWLEDGMENTS

We acknowledge the following positive individuals who helped make *The Leadership Pill* a reality through their collective and sustained integrity, partnership, and affirmation: Fred Hills, editor and wise soul of Free Press at Simon & Schuster, and Margret McBride, for catching the initial excitement of the book; Richard Andrews, Humberto Medina, Dottie Hamilt, Anna Espino, Martha Lawrence, and the Best-Seller Marketing Team at The Ken Blanchard Companies; Jerome Althea and Sylvester McBean for their inspiration; Lauren Keith, Steve Jensen, Pam Johnson, Ron and Sherri Muchnick, Mark and Maxine Rossman, Mo M. Morris, Steve Z., Johnny and Junior Schraibman, Ryan Sherpco, Dr. Lawrence Hier III, Tim Haggstrom, Sal Bernstein, Chayks, Moshe Maoz, the esteemed members of the Skaneateles Country Club, and others who served as critical reviewers.

In addition, we acknowledge those individuals who have worked with Ken and whose ideas have subsequently enhanced Marc's thinking as well, including Margie Blanchard, Ichak Adizes, Jim Ballard, Sheldon Bowles, Hal Burrows, Don Carew, Eunice Parisi-Carew, John Carlos, Garry Demarest, Chris Edmonds, Fred Finch, Susan Fowler, Bob Glaser, Laurie Hawkins, Paul Hersey, Phil Hodges, Bill Hybels, Spencer Johnson, Thad Lacinak, Robert Lorber, Michael O'Connor, William Oncken, Jr., Norman Vincent Peale, Alan Randolph, Dana and Jim Robinson, Don Shula, Chuck Tompkins, Terry Waghorn, Drea Zigarmi, and Pat Zigarmi, among others.

We are grateful to all of you and give you our heartfelt thanks!

ABOUT THE AUTHORS

Ken Blanchard is chairman of the board of The Ken Blanchard Companies, a worldwide training and development firm. He is the author of a dozen best-selling books—including the blockbuster international best-seller *The One Minute Manager®* and the giant business best-sellers *Whale Done!, Raving Fans,* and *Gung Ho!*—which have combined sales of more than fifteen million copies in more than twenty-five languages. Few people have made a more positive and lasting impact on the day-to-day management of people and companies as has Ken Blanchard. He and his wife, Margie, live in San Diego and work with their son Scott, daughter Debbie, and her husband Humberto Medina.

Marc Muchnick is founder and president of People First Group and author of *Naked Management: Bare Essentials for Motivating the X-Generation at Work.* He is an internationally known motivational speaker, leadership expert, and online management professor with featured appearances on CNN and in major business journals. Marc attributes the true start of his professional career to working for The Ken Blanchard Companies while completing his Ph.D. in industrial-organizational psychology. He has been active in the Big Brothers Program for more than twelve years and lives in San Diego with his wife Kim, children Jessica and Blake, and dog Scruffy.

SERVICES AVAILABLE

In 1979 Ken Blanchard founded The Ken Blanchard Companies to support organizations looking to put the principles of his books into practice. Now a major international management consultancy and training organization, the company works with many of the world's leading businesses to unleash the full power and potential of their people. The Ken Blanchard Companies is perhaps best known as the originator of the most widely used leadership development process, Situational Leadership® II and also specializes in Team Building, Organizational Change and Customer Service. Consultancy services, in-house training, public workshops, coaching, speakers and a wide variety of learning materials are also provided through a network of offices in 30 countries worldwide. If The Leadership Pill has inspired you to transform your business, contact:

The Ken Blanchard Companies

United Kingdom
Blanchard House
1 Graham Road
Wimbledon
London SW19 3SW

Tel: +44 (0) 20 8540 5404
Fax: +44 (0) 20 8540 5464
Email: uk@kenblanchard.com

USA
125 State Place
Escondido
California 92029

Tel: (001) 760 489 5005
Fax: (001) 760 489 8407

For other worldwide locations see page 116

People First Group, founded by Marc Muchnick in the early 1990s, provides cutting-edge services in the areas of motivational speaking, experiential skill building, organizational and team assessment, and performance coaching to Fortune 500 companies and other top organizations around the world. Credited with its innovative focus on leadership, attracting and retaining talent, managing and motivating Generations X and Y, team building, self-motivation, and navigating through change, People First Group is a proven leader in helping organizations recognize the power of motivating, developing, and valuing their people.

People First Group, LLC

13354 Grandvia Point
San Diego, CA 92130
Tel: (001) 858 259 1228
www.peoplefirstgroup.com

FURTHER INTERNATIONAL AFFILIATES

Australia
The PTD Group Pty. Ltd.
Paul Stapleton
PO 374
Eastwood NSW
2122
Tel: 61 2 9858 2822
Fax: 61 2 9858 2844
Email: ptd@ptd.com.au

Ireland
Blanchard Ireland
Morgan Pierse, Director
Brookfield House
Carysfort Ave
Blackrock
Dublin
Tel: 353 1 283 3500
Fax: 353 1 283 3592
Email: morgpier@iol.ie

Netherlands
Blanchard Nederland
Cor Van De Schoot, Director
Zandweg 35
3544 AA
Utrecht
Tel: 3130-666-1715
Fax: 3130-666-1315
Email: btd@wxs.nl

New Zealand
The Blanchard International
Group, NZ
Malcolm Sutherland, Managing
Director
Level 7 Presence House
57-59 Courtenay Place
P.O. Box 6549, Marion Square
Wellington
Tel: 644-385-9763
Fax: 644-385-9232
Email: malcolm.sutherland@
blanchard.co.nz

Sweden
Blanchard, Sweden
Jan Ericsson, General Manager
Box 1212
SE-181 24 LIDINGÖ
Stockholm
Tel: 46-8-587 731 00
Fax: 46-8-587 731 99
Email: jan.ericsson@blanchard.se